Happy 10th Birthday

Made in the USA
Coppell, TX
12 December 2020

44355975R00069